AN OUTDOORS PUZZLE BOOK

Alan Jamieson

CASTLES,
CHURCHES
AND HOUSES

Illustrated by Philip Page

PUFFIN BOOKS

Puffin Books, Penguin Books Ltd, Harmondsworth,
Middlesex, England
Penguin Books, 625 Madison Avenue,
New York, New York 10022, U.S.A.
Penguin Books Australia Ltd, Ringwood,
Victoria, Australia
Penguin Books Canada Ltd, 2801 John Street,
Markham, Ontario, Canada L3R 1B4
Penguin Books (N.Z.) Ltd, 182–190 Wairau Road,
Auckland 10, New Zealand

First published 1981

Made and printed in Great Britain by
Richard Clay (The Chaucer Press) Ltd, Bungay, Suffolk
Set in Monotype Plantin

Contents

1 HOW TO USE THIS BOOK

This book will help you when you are out and about looking at *buildings*. Take the book with you when you travel around. It has drawings and pictures which show you the different kinds of buildings you may see. There are quiz questions on castles, forts, churches, cathedrals, historic houses and buildings in towns. The book will help you to spot and to recognize these buildings, or their ruins and remains.

Try the picture-quizzes and the word-quizzes out on your family and friends. They will test their knowledge and their skill.

Keep your score
The answers and a score-sheet are at the back of the book. Keep the score for each page or for a section of the book.

Keep a record
There are boxes for you to tick when you visit a particular place, and write-in spaces for you to keep a record of the places you visit.

Have fun – and add to your knowledge!

Chapter 2.

1. a barrow ✓
2. trackways ✓
3. the gatehouse ✗ keep
4. the Tower of London. ✓

$\frac{3}{4}$

2 DISCOVERING THE PAST

Ruined castles and abbeys, palaces once lived in by kings and queens, market crosses and coaching inns – the evidence of history is all around you. Each year, tens of thousands of people visit Britain's castles, cathedrals, historic houses and old towns. They try to imagine what it was like to live there hundreds of years ago. What was it really like to live in a Roman fort, an abbey, a great house or a castle?

History is about people, but it is also about places. All over Britain there are ruined castles, old towns and historic houses which attract thousands of visitors. And, of course, there are buildings still very much in use – churches, cathedrals, inns, guildhalls, factories and so on. Have you looked closely at the buildings in *your* town or village? They can tell you a lot – if you know how to read them.

This book with its picture puzzles and quizzes will test your knowledge – and your skill – in seeing if you can recognize parts of old buildings when you see them. As well as keeping you amused and on your toes, you should learn a lot from this book so that the next time you look at an old building – or a new one – you will see it with fresh eyes.

Ruins and remains

The book starts off with pictures of the buildings erected by the earliest people to have lived in Britain. Using tools made from stone, bronze and iron, they built temples, forts and walled strongholds.

Here is a short quiz to get you started.

1 What is the word used to describe a mound of earth or stones covering an ancient burial place – is it a moat, or a barrow, or a fort?

2 In order to travel from one village to another, the ancient Britons used paths which ran along the tops of the hills, so avoiding the thick forests in the valleys below. What name is now used to describe these paths – roads, streets, avenues or trackways?

3 What is the word used to describe the great stone building which was the strongest part of a medieval castle – is it the gatehouse, the bailey or the keep?

4 Which of these famous castles was built by order of William the Conqueror: Harlech Castle, the Tower of London, or Windsor Castle?

3 RUINS OF LONG AGO

Spread across the countryside are the ruins and remains of places once lived in by people long ago. There are earth mounds from the Stone Age; temples, hillforts and barrows (burial chambers) from the Stone, Bronze and Iron Ages; and all kinds of ruins – walls, camps, towns, villas, temples and so on – from Roman times.

Can you name these famous and mysterious places? The clues should help you.

1 A temple, where people once worshipped the sun and strange gods. It was built over 3,500 years ago in southern Britain.

s t o n e h e n g e

2 Built by the Romans to be the northern frontier of the province of Britain.

H a d r i a n's
w a l l

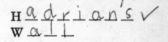

3 This man-made mound is in Wiltshire. It is thought to have been built about 4,000 years ago. What it is remains a mystery – a burial mound for a king perhaps?

s I L B U R Y
H I L L

4 Built by the Romans and called by them *Aquae Sulis*, this town had villas, baths and temples.

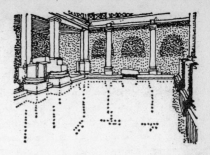

B _a t h_

5 Cut from a chalk hillside by the Atrebates, an Iron Age tribe which lived in southern Britain.

The W _h i t e_
H _o r s e_
of Uff _i n g t o n_

$\frac{4}{6}$

6 This circle of standing stones in Wiltshire was set up about 5,000 years ago by people of the Bronze Age.

A _V E_ b _U R_ y

Long barrows and round barrows

Long barrows were mounds of earth and stones built about 5,000 years ago. They were used in the Stone and Bronze Ages as houses for the dead. You can sometimes see round barrows in the middle of a field, although they show up best in air photographs. Often the barrows have been damaged by ploughing and all you can see now is a chalky patch against the dark soil of a field or a difference in the colour or height of the vegetation (a *cropmark*).

A good book which lists long barrows (and round barrows) throughout Britain is *Collins Field Guide to Archaeology* by Eric S. Wood.

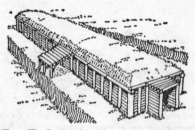

Reconstruction of Fussell's Lodge long barrow in Wiltshire

Round barrows were used as burial chambers for the dead. There are about 10,000 to 20,000 round barrows in Britain. The bodies were often buried with tools, weapons and food to help in the next life. Round barrows (often called *tumuli* on Ordnance Survey maps) can be found in most parts of Britain, although many have been badly damaged or have disappeared completely.

I saw a round barrow or *tumulus* at <u>Caernarvon Castle</u>

A round barrow

8

Iron Age hillforts

These forts were built by the Celts or ancient Britons to defend themselves against other tribes. When the Romans and, later, the Saxons invaded Britain, the hillforts were used again.

Two famous hillforts are at Maiden Castle in Dorset and at Cadbury Castle in Somerset.

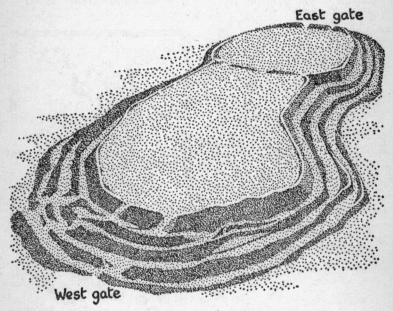

East gate

West gate

Maiden Castle, near Dorchester in Dorset

A quick quiz

1 How many earth banks are there in this hillfort?
2 How many ditches are there?
3 How many gates are there?

I'm not counting this.

Put a tick here if you have visited these forts.
    Maiden Castle ☑
    Cadbury Castle ☑

I saw a hillfort at *Maiden Castle.*

The Romans

The Romans built forts, camps, towns, roads, villas and walls. As you go round the countryside, you may see evidence of the Roman occupation.

Here are some pictures of Roman remains. But what are they?

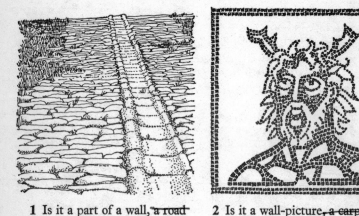

1 Is it a part of a wall, ~~a road or a market square?~~

2 Is it a wall-picture, ~~a carpet or a tile-floor?~~

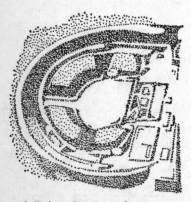

3 Is it a theatre, ~~a fort or a market?~~

4 Is it a wall-tower, ~~a shop or Roman baths?~~

Roman forts

Forts and fortresses built by the Romans were rectangular, rather like the shape of a playing-card. On the outside of the fort were thick walls, with two or more gates. The Romans added towers or *bastions* to strengthen the outer walls. Inside were barracks for the troops, granaries to store their food supplies, bath-houses, stables and offices.

Portchester in Hampshire was a Roman fort built at the end of the third century (about AD 280). It was used as a garrison for soldiers defending the south coast of Britain from Saxon sea-raiders. Many hundreds of years later the Normans built a castle inside the old Roman walls and added a church.

Here is a drawing of Portchester fort as it is today. Some of the labels (descriptions) of the various parts are missing. From the box at the bottom of the page, choose words that fit into the drawing.

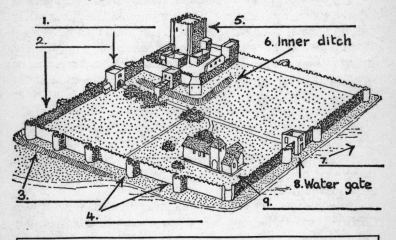

1.
2.
3.
4.
5.
6. Inner ditch
7.
8. Water gate
9.

| harbour | outer ditch | bastions | outer wall |
| main gate | twelfth-century church | twelfth-century keep |

Look for a fort

I saw the ruins of a Roman fort at _____

I noted these parts of the fort _____

11

4 CASTLES AND FORTS

Who built the first castles in Britain? It really depends on what we mean by a 'castle'. The Romans built the first forts and fortresses, such as those at York, Gloucester, Lincoln and other places; they also built a fort at Portchester on the south coast, to protect Britain from the attacks of Saxon sea-raiders.

The Normans were probably the first people to build the large fortified houses and fortresses we now call 'castles'. The earliest ones were surrounded by a ditch, with a wooden fence on a high bank just inside it, and huts on the open space in the middle. This space was called the bailey.

In the twelfth century, the Normans added to these castles by building an outer stone wall, and by erecting a large stone keep within the bailey. The castles now looked really strong, with a moat, high surrounding walls, towers, a keep and a bailey.

The castles built in the thirteenth century by the engineers of Edward I were very different. To keep the wild Welshmen under control, Edward made the towns of Conway and Caernarvon into fortresses, with the castle part of, and dominating, the town. Other strong castles, such as Harlech and Beaumaris, had one ring or circle of defences inside another. These therefore came to be called *concentric* castles.

Later on, cannons were used to smash down the walls of the castles. This seemed to bring their usefulness to an end but they weren't finished yet. King Henry VIII's engineers widened the moats and strengthened the outer walls. But by the time of Queen Elizabeth I, the landowners and the nobles had left most of the old castles to live in more comfortable houses.

Castles became very useful again during the Civil War between Charles I and Parliament. Some were besieged and were only captured after bombardment by cannon fire.

Today, you have to use your imagination when you visit the ruins of these once mighty castles. Think about attacking a castle, and about defending it. Think what it was like to live there during a cold winter or a long siege. Look at the castle to see if it has a dungeon, where the kitchens are placed, if it had a moat, draw-bridge, portcullis and other defences. Think about how you would attack it, supposing you were the general commanding the army outside the walls.

Name the castles

Can you name these castles? The clues should help.

1 Built by William
the Conqueror, it
has the famous
Traitors' Gate.

The T O W E R o F
L O N D O N

2 A castle with a
round tower, it is
outside London and
is one of the homes
of the Royal
Family.

W I N D S O R
C A S T L E

3 Beside the
Thames, it was one
of the favourite
castles and homes
of King Henry VIII.

H a m p t o n
C O U R T

4 A castle in a
Scottish city,
besieged many
times by English
armies.

E D I N B U R G H
C A S T L E

Famous castles

Match up the castle with the description of it or what happened there. The castles are all in the box at the bottom of the page.

1 Mary, Queen of Scots, was held prisoner in this Scottish castle. She escaped across the lake in a rowing boat.

Loch Leven ✓

2 Called 'the Key to England', this Kent castle can be seen from France on a clear day.

Dover ✓

3 It took from 1283 to 1327 to build this Welsh castle, which was the setting for the investiture of the Prince of Wales in 1969.

Caernarvon ✓

4 In this Gloucestershire castle, King Edward II was murdered in 1327.

Carisbrooke ✗

5 In this castle on the Isle of Wight, King Charles I was held prisoner in 1647.

Goodrich ✗

6 This castle stands above the river Wye with a commanding view of the border lands between England and Wales.

Berkeley ✗

7 Mary, Queen of Scots, and King James VI were crowned in this castle which has been called 'the gateway to the Highlands'.

Stirling ✓

8 This castle in Kent was attacked by the army of King John in 1215. The King's soldiers mined beneath the walls of the castle, so forcing the garrison to surrender.

20 points $\frac{5}{8}$

Rochester ✓

Stirling	**Goodrich**	**Dover**	**Berkeley**
Carisbrooke	**Rochester**	**Loch Leven**	**Caernarvon**

White Castle

White Castle, once called Llantilio Castle, in Gwent, was built in the twelfth century and enlarged later. It has many of the features of stone castles built on the border of England and Wales, and of castles in other parts of Britain.

You have to name *six* parts of this castle. The names are all in the box at the bottom of the page. Fill them in on the picture in the places that have been left for you.

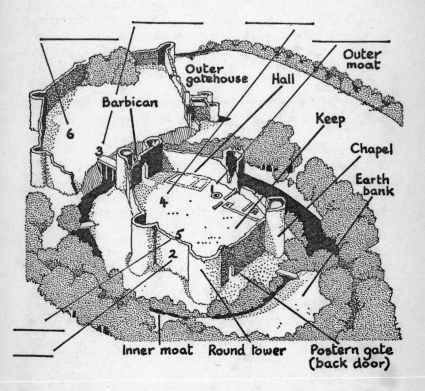

| outer bailey | battlements | well |
| inner bailey | drawbridge | curtain wall |

15

Attack! Attack!

Harlech Castle in Wales was built 700 years ago by order of King Edward I. The castle stands on a rock overlooking the sea. It has a strong gatehouse, a 'curtain wall' with four towers, and other defences. Ships could sail right up to the water-gate to unload supplies of food, so making sure that the garrison would never go hungry.

In 1401, Owain Glyndwr, the famous Welsh leader, attacked Harlech Castle. After a siege that lasted four years, the garrison was bribed to surrender to the Welsh soldiers patiently waiting outside. But seven years later, the English were back. A thousand men, equipped with siege towers and cannons, attacked the castle. Eventually the Welsh soldiers, weary and starving, had to surrender to the English army.

Look at the drawing opposite of the siege of Harlech Castle. Some things are missing. Add the following to the drawing:

1 English ships arriving in the harbour
2 cannons firing against the walls of the castle
3 soldiers trying to cross the bridge to the gatehouse
4 Welsh bowmen on the castle walls firing at the English
5 a trebuchet (a kind of artillery piece which could fling stones a long distance) firing at another wall

Harlech Castle today

16

Harlech Castle under siege

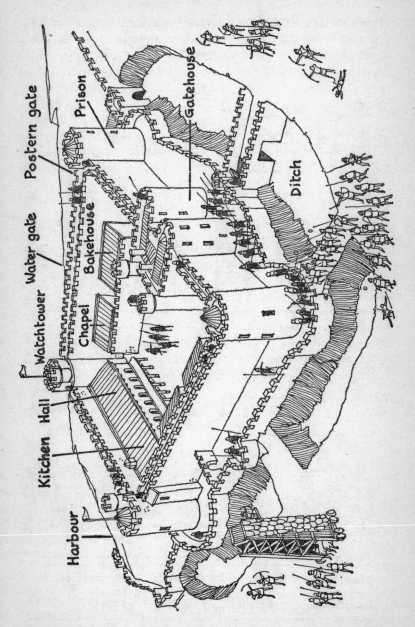

Postern gate · Prison · Gatehouse · Ditch · Water gate · Watchtower · Bakehouse · Chapel · Kitchen · Hall · Harbour

Castle spotting

First of all, choose the words from the box at the bottom of the page to match the drawings. Then put a tick in the square when you visit any castle and see the particular part. In the space write the name of the castle where you saw it.

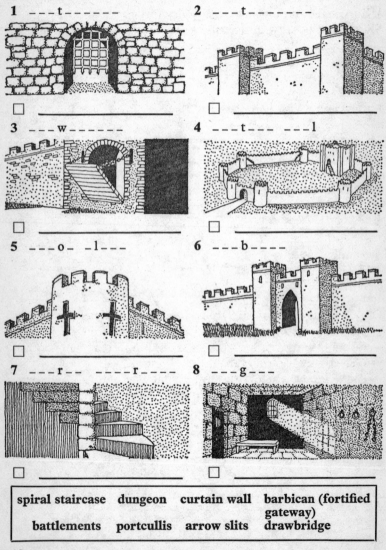

1 _ _ _ t _ _ _ _ _ _

2 _ _ _ t _ _ _ _ _ _

□ _____

□ _____

3 _ _ _ w _ _ _ _ _ _

4 _ _ _ t _ _ _   _ _ _ l

□ _____

□ _____

5 _ _ _ o _   _ l _ _ _

6 _ _ _ b _ _ _ _

□ _____

□ _____

7 _ _ _ r _ _   _ _ _ _ r _ _ _ _

8 _ _ _ g _ _ _

□ _____

□ _____

| spiral staircase | dungeon | curtain wall | barbican (fortified gateway) |
| battlements | portcullis | arrow slits | drawbridge |

18

Keeping a record

As you travel about the countryside, keep a record of the castles you visit. In your notebook, make a list of all the castles, forts, ruins or castle-mounds which you see. You could keep a short-hand record like this:

MB could stand for motte and bailey castles.

SK could be used to describe a shell-keep, such as Restormel Castle in Cornwall.

What abbreviations would you use to describe the following castles?

1 a tower-keep such as Rochester in Kent

2 a many-sided tower like the polygonal keep at Orford Castle in Suffolk

3 a curtain wall castle like Conway in Wales

4 a fortified manor house like Stokesay in Salop

5 a keep and high-walled castle like Dover Castle in Kent

The keep at Rochester

Draw a map of Britain and Ireland and on it mark all the castles you can find in books or maps. You can get books from the library with lists of castles. But it may be more fun to start with castles you have visited or know about.

There are many books on castles. One that you will find very useful is the *List and Map of Historic Monuments*, published by the Department of the Environment. You can buy it from Government (HMSO) bookshops or ordinary booksellers. It lists most of the castles and shows you where they are on the map. Here are some other useful books on castles.

Discovering Castles in England and Wales by John Kinross (Shire Publications)

The Castle Story by Sheila Sancha (Kestrel)

Castles in England and Wales by W. D. Simpson (Batsford)

The Zebra Book of Castles by Plantagenet Somerset Fry (Evans)

5 CHURCHES AND CATHEDRALS

Almost every town or village has a church. Some churches are over a thousand years old, and contain many clues about the way people worshipped in the past.

What do you know about churches? Can you name the different parts of a church? Here is a quiz to get you started. The answers are in the box at the bottom of the page.

PEWS

1 What is the name for the table or bench, usually covered with an embroidered cloth, which is the most sacred part of the church?

CHANCEL

2 What is the raised platform from which the vicar or preacher gives the sermon?

BRASSES

3 What are the wooden bench seats, sometimes with high backs, for the congregation to sit on?

PULPIT

4 What is the name for the part of the church for the people or congregation?

NAVE

5 What is the name for the part of the church where the choir sits?

SCREEN

6 What was the special wooden partition added to churches in the fourteenth and fifteenth centuries which separated the choir and priest's section from the rest of the church?

ORGAN

7 What musical instrument, made from hundreds of small pipes, is often to be found in a parish church?

ALTAR

8 What are the pieces of metal set into stone (often with the figure of a knight or his wife) which are memorials to people who have died?

3/8

chancel	brasses	screen	organ
nave	pews	altar	pulpit

The explorer's guide

Can you name these parts of a church? Match the words in the box at the bottom of the page to the pictures.

When you visit a church and look for the different parts of it, put a tick in the box to show you have seen it. In the space, write the name of the church (St John's, for example) and where it is.

1 roofs of stone with arched ceilings

☑ _fan vaults_

2 images of dead people carved on top of the slabs covering their graves

☑ _effigies_

3 a reading desk usually made of wood or brass on which the Bible is placed

☑ _lectern_

4 a stone or wooden partition dividing the *nave* (where the people sit) from the *chancel* (where the choir sits)

☑ _screen_

5 it holds the water used in baptism

☒ _piscina_

6 a shallow stone basin with a drain, used to wash the *chalice* (cup) and the plate after the Holy Communion service

☑ _font_

$\frac{4}{6}$

effigies	**screen**
piscina	**fan vaults**
lectern	**font**

Name the parts of a church

The drawing shows the outside of a parish church. Match the names of the different parts of the church in the box to the numbers on the picture.

tower	gargoyle	yew tree
pinnacle	belfry	churchyard
weather-vane	porch	buttress
west door	churchyard cross	lych-gate
scratch-dial	parapet	gravestone

Keeping a record

When you visit a church or a cathedral, keep a record of the special things you see. For instance, some churches have openings cut at an angle through a wall or pillar. These are called *squints* and they were made so that people in the side aisles could have a clear view of the altar.

Here is a list of some of the different parts of a church. Tick the boxes when you see them. In the space, write the name of the church and where it is.

1 *squint* ☐ _____

2 *sanctuary lamp*   Lamps were hung in the area of the church called the sanctuary, a place in front of the altar.
☐ _____

3 *stoup*   A kind of basin set into a niche in the wall and near the main door. It contained the water blessed by the priest. People dipped their fingers into it and made the sign of the Cross.
☐ _____

4 *banners*   They are often beautifully embroidered and hang in the church when not being used in church processions.
☐ _____

5 *sedilia*   Three or four seats beside the altar for the priest, the deacons (who read the Gospels and the Epistles) and the clerk.
☐ _____

6 *stained glass windows*   Sometimes with scenes from the Old Testament or from the life of Jesus.   ☐ _____

7 *iron-bound chest*   Used in the Middle Ages to collect money for the poor.   ☐ _____

8 *brasses*   Usually in the figure of a knight and his wife, set into the walls or the floor of the church.   ☐ _____

9 *reredos*   An ornamental screen, often carved in wood, set up behind the altar.   ☐ _____

10 *tithe barn*   Used to store corn when the people of the parish had to pay a *tithe* (a tenth of their produce) to the church.
☐ _____

Make a list of other things you have seen in a church.
chapel, cloisters.

Spot the cathedral

A cathedral is the main church in a church district called a *diocese*. A bishop has his throne here. The word *cathedra* means a throne or chair. In Britain you will see many beautiful cathedrals with different styles of architecture. Here are drawings of some famous cathedrals.

Where are they? The clues should help you.

1 Built by Sir Christopher Wren and completed in 1710.

St Paul's, London

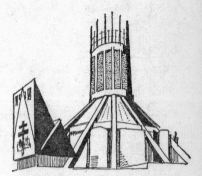

2 This twentieth-century Roman Catholic cathedral has a sixteen-sided lantern tower.

Liverpool

3 This fifteenth-century Scottish cathedral has a spire over 160 feet (49 metres) high.

St Gile's, Edinburgh

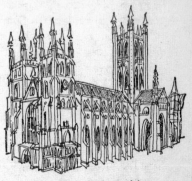

4 The oldest cathedral in England, it contains the shrine to St Thomas à Becket.

Canterbury

5 This cathedral in Wiltshire has the tallest spire (404 feet, 123 metres) in England.

Salisbury

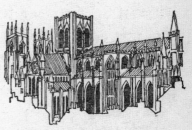

6 This new cathedral was designed by Sir Basil Spence and opened in 1965.

Coventry

7 This cathedral in Somerset has a beautiful, richly covered west front.

Wells

8 This cathedral in Yorkshire has five great windows called the Five Sisters.

York

$\frac{8}{8}$ *

Keep a record of the cathedrals you visit.

I have been to these cathedrals:

1   _Lincoln_
2   _Durham_
3   _York_
4   _Ely._

25

Windows

Windows provide many clues to help you to spot when a church or cathedral was built. At first, the thick-walled Saxon and Norman churches had little more than slits for windows. Then the style changed. Windows became larger with wider openings and less heavy stonework. In some churches and cathedrals built in the fifteenth century, the whole of one wall seems to be made of glass, with thin stone bars between the panes of glass.

Here are some windows from different periods of history. Draw a line from the window to the style of architecture in the middle.

1 windows were small with round or triangular arches

Saxon ✓

Saxon

Perpendicular

Early English Gothic

Decorated

Norman

2 high glass arches with a decorative pattern of ornamental stonework to support the glass

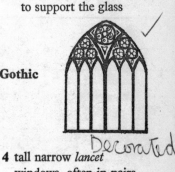

✓

Decorated

3 rounded arches with mouldings in a chevron pattern

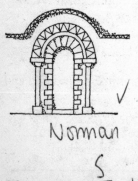

✓

Norman

4 tall narrow *lancet* windows, often in pairs sharply pointed at the top

5 more glass, and with criss-crossing stone columns and bars

✓ E. English Gothic

Perpendicular

$\frac{5}{5}$ *

Where did you see them?

Keep a record of the churches you see as you travel around. Here is a list to help you. Tick the box and write the name of the church in the space when you see one.

1 Saxon churches built possibly in the tenth century.

☐ _____

2 Norman churches built after 1066 with square or round towers.

☐ _____

a Saxon tower

3 medieval churches built in various styles with towers or spires.

☐ _____

4 sixteenth- and seventeenth-century churches.

☐ _____

5 classical eighteenth-century churches such as St Martin-in-the-Fields in London.

☐ _____

a medieval church

6 nineteenth-century churches built in a style similar to the medieval period.

☐ _____

7 Methodist chapels in Wales and elsewhere.

☐ _____

a classical eighteenth-century church

8 twentieth-century churches.

☐ _____

There are many books to help you find out about churches and cathedrals. Here is a list of some of them.

Guide to English Parish Churches by John Betjeman (Collins)
The Observer's Book of Churches (Warne)
Discovering Churches by John Harries (Shire Publications)
The Observer's Book of Cathedrals (Warne)

6 ABBEYS AND PRIORIES

In the Middle Ages, men and women gave up a normal way of life in order to live in a monastery or a nunnery. There they spent their time in prayer, study and work. Most of the buildings of the monasteries were destroyed at the time of the Reformation in the sixteenth century, although there are some monasteries still in existence today. There are also fine abbey churches still in use, such as Bath and Westminster.

It is possible to visit the ruins of some of the ancient monasteries and to imagine what life was like in them hundreds of years ago. Among them are Rievaulx Abbey in North Yorkshire, Tintern Abbey in Gwent, Dryburgh Abbey in Scotland and many others.

Here is a monastery quiz to start you off.

1 Who was the head of an abbey or a monastery – a monk, an abbot or a bishop?
2 Which saints were the founders of these Orders?
    a the Dominican friars (the Blackfriars)
    b the Benedictine monks (the Black Monks)
    c the Franciscan friars (the Greyfriars)
3 What was the name of the monk who trained the other monks to sing – the sacristan, the prior or the cantor?
4 What do you think these rooms were for?
    a the dorter
    b the cellarium
5 What was the name for the young men who were training to be monks – beginners, novices or reserves?
6 What was the name for the men who were not full monks although they lived in the monastery and did the everyday work there – lay brothers, friars or guests?
7 At about six o'clock in the morning, the monks attended their first service of the day. What was the service called – Vigils, Prime or High Mass?
8 The monks wrote out their books by hand, sometimes adding little pictures done in coloured inks. What was the word (which in Latin means 'written by hand') for these handwritten books – picture-books, parchments or manuscripts?

Monasteries: what to look for

In the box at the bottom of this page are the names of different parts of a monastery. Match the names to the descriptions.

1 A room where the business of the monastery was conducted and where the Abbot read from the Bible.

2 A square with four covered sides, used by the monks for walking, thinking and study.

3 Small compartments built into the walls of the cloister where monks could read and write.

4 A room from which one of the monks gave away food and clothing to poor people.

5 A room where monks met people from outside the monastery to talk and give advice.

6 The hospital where old and sick people were looked after by the monks.

7 In this part of the monastery the porter was always on duty.

8 The room where the monks ate their meals.

9 The long room where the monks slept.

10 A room where the monks could be sure to find a good fire blazing.

refectory	carrels	gatehouse
warming room	cloisters	almonry
chapter house	dormitory	parlour
	infirmary	

Fountains Abbey

Fountains Abbey in Yorkshire was a Cistercian abbey founded in 1132. At first the monks led a simple life of work and prayer but later on they became very rich from the profits of sheep farming. With their money, they built a beautiful church within the monastery, which is now in ruins.

Parts of the Abbey are numbered. Match the numbers to the parts.

dining hall or refectory	church
chapter house	kitchen
cloisters	infirmary hall
dormitory for the lay brothers	

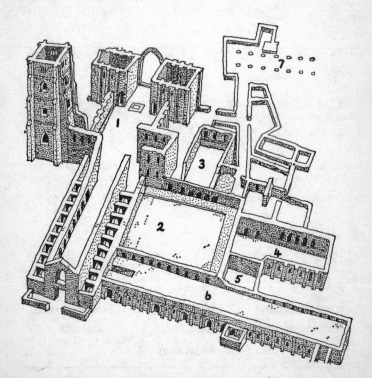

The explorer's guide

Try to visit the sites of abbeys and priories. When you go, make a plan of the buildings. The guidebook to the site will be a great help.

What are the names for these parts of an abbey? The names are in the centre of the page.

abbot's kitchen

night stairs

pulpit

nave

crypt

cloisters

Keeping a record Bath,

I saw abbeys at ~~Bolton~~ Rievaulx

There are many good guidebooks on abbeys. Here are two:
Abbeys: An Introduction (HMSO)
Discovering Abbeys and Priories by G. N. Wright (Shire
  Publications)

7 HISTORIC HOUSES

Throughout Britain there are historic houses or 'stately homes' which for one reason or another are famous. There are many other houses, castles and gardens which are not so well known. Have you ever visited one or more of these houses?

Over ten million people visit the castles, houses and gardens of Britain each year. There are lots of things to see and do there. In the first place, the houses are sometimes built on a magnificent site overlooking the sea, or a lake or a town. They may be surrounded by beautiful gardens or parkland. Some owners have added nature trails, or a safari park, amusements, shops and shows. At Beaulieu in Hampshire there is a famous Motor Museum of old cars, buses and motor-cycles. Inside the houses there is usually much to look at and to learn. Sometimes there are whole rooms set out exactly as they were hundreds of years ago. The rooms are often packed with valuable and rare furniture, pictures, china and books. Some houses have kitchens laid out with cooking utensils used many years ago.

This section is about these houses. Here is a short quiz to get you started.

1 Which of these famous houses is a family home owned by the Queen: Woburn Abbey, Beaulieu Abbey, Sandringham or Durham Castle?
2 Which one of these houses and palaces in London was once the home of the Duke of Wellington and is now a museum: Hampton Court Palace, Apsley House, St James's Palace or Kensington Palace?
3 Which of these famous architects (who all built houses and homes) built St Paul's Cathedral in London: Inigo Jones, John Nash, Robert Adam or Christopher Wren?
4 One of Britain's greatest Prime Ministers lived at Chartwell in Kent. Who was he?
5 What was the name of the first President of the USA whose ancestors once lived at Sulgrave Manor in Oxfordshire?
6 Cawdor Castle in Scotland is famous because William Shakespeare wrote a play about a Scottish lord who murdered King Duncan at the Castle and then became King of Scotland himself. What was the name of this Scottish lord?

Historic houses – a picture quiz

In this picture quiz, match the house or castle to the picture.

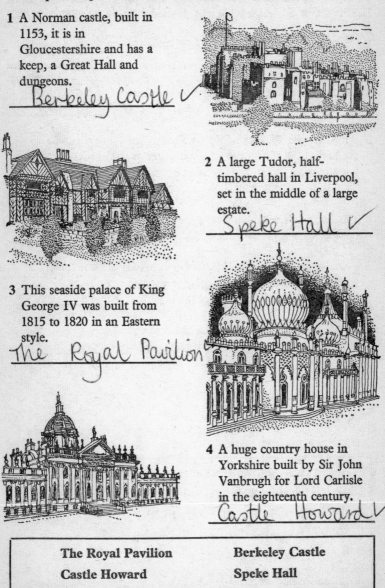

1 A Norman castle, built in 1153, it is in Gloucestershire and has a keep, a Great Hall and dungeons.

Berkeley Castle ✓

2 A large Tudor, half-timbered hall in Liverpool, set in the middle of a large estate.

Speke Hall ✓

3 This seaside palace of King George IV was built from 1815 to 1820 in an Eastern style.

The Royal Pavilion

4 A huge country house in Yorkshire built by Sir John Vanbrugh for Lord Carlisle in the eighteenth century.

Castle Howard ✓

The Royal Pavilion	Berkeley Castle
Castle Howard	Speke Hall

4/4 *

Famous folk and famous homes

Some houses are famous because of the people who once lived there. Here is a quiz about them. Match the houses to the people or events.

1 Home of the Duke of Marlborough where Sir Winston Churchill was born.

Hatfield House ✗

2 Once the home of Anne Boleyn before she met and married King Henry VIII.

Blenheim ✗

3 Built between 1607 and 1611 by Robert Cecil, the Earl of Salisbury, the Chief Minister to King James I, it has been the family home of the Cecils ever since then.

Palace.

Hever Castle ✗

4 The home of Sir Walter Scott, the famous novelist who wrote *Ivanhoe* and *Rob Roy*.

Abbotsford. ✓

5 The thatched cottage at Stratford-upon-Avon where the wife of William Shakespeare lived before she married him.

Ann Hathaway's cottage ✓

6 The home of the Dukes of Bedford for over 300 years, it is surrounded by a huge park.

Woburn Abbey ✓

$\frac{3}{6}$

Ann Hathaway's Cottage, Warwickshire ✗
Woburn Abbey, Bedfordshire ✓
Hatfield House, Hertfordshire ✗
Blenheim Palace, Oxfordshire ✗
Abbotsford, Scotland ✗
Hever Castle, Kent ✗

Where are they?

In the box at the bottom of the page are the names of ten of the most visited houses in Britain. But where are they? Write their names in the correct places on the map.

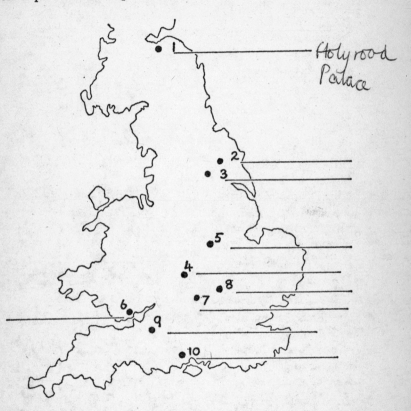

1 ———————— *Holyrood Palace*

2 ————————————

3 ————————————

5 ————————————

4 ————————————

8 ————————————

7 ————————————

6 ————————————

9 ————————————

10 ———————————

Holyrood Palace, Edinburgh	Harewood House, West Yorkshire
Blenheim Palace, Oxfordshire	
Woburn Abbey, Bedfordshire	Castle Howard, North Yorkshire
Longleat House, Wiltshire	
Beaulieu, Hampshire	Cardiff Castle
Belvoir Castle, Leicestershire	Warwick Castle

Pick and match

The pictures show some famous houses. Complete the puzzle of the name of the house.

1 On the Isle of Wight, this was Queen Victoria's favourite country house, partly designed by Prince Albert, her husband.

O s h o r n e
H o u s e

2 According to William Shakespeare's *Macbeth* King Duncan of Scotland was murdered here. In the seventeenth century, the mansion was rebuilt in the style of a French château.

G l a m i s
c a s t l e

3 An Elizabethan mansion in Wiltshire, home of the Marquess of Bath, it now has a safari park, with lions roaming in it.

L o n g l e a t
H o u s e

4 This magnificent mansion is in Derbyshire. It is the home of the Duke of Devonshire and it contains a great collection of books, furniture and pictures.

c h a t s w o r t h ✓

Abbeys, castles and homes

Some historic houses now owned by the National Trust or by private owners were once abbeys (like Woburn Abbey), royal palaces, barons' castles, inns, or homes of well-known people.

This puzzle tests your knowledge of houses and castles. The answers are in the box.

1 It was built by Cardinal Wolsey and presented by him to King Henry VIII to be used as a royal palace near to the Thames.
2 Once the home of William Wordsworth, it is in Grasmere, Cumbria. Wordsworth lived here with his sister and had ideas for many of his poems on walks around the countryside.
3 A great castle, built by order of King Edward I in the fourteenth century to keep the Welsh under control. It has been lived in continuously for 660 years and among the famous people who stayed here were the Earl of Leicester (one of Queen Elizabeth I's courtiers) and King Charles I.
4 Once a monastery, it was built in Dorset in the twelfth century by Cistercian monks and 400 years later it was converted into a private home.
5 A baron's fortress in Northumberland, built and owned by the Percy family. The thick stone walls and the dungeon were often needed during the Border wars between England and Scotland.

1 _____

2 _____

3 _____

4 _____

5 _____

Alnwick Castle
Dove Cottage
Chirk Castle
Forde Abbey
Hampton Court

Many properties are looked after by the National Trust, which has a section for young people. The National Trust has a list of the buildings it owns, obtainable from their offices, The National Trust, 42 Queen Anne's Gate, London SW1H 9AS and The National Trust for Scotland, 5 Charlotte Square, Edinburgh EH2 4DU.

8 HOUSES AND HOMES

When you walk around your own town or village, or one that you visit on holiday, keep your eyes open. The buildings will tell you a lot about the history of the town. And if you can recognize the different kinds of buildings, and the materials used to construct them, you will find your visit a lot more interesting.

Let's start with *houses*. Your town may be a modern one, and at first the houses may seem to be much the same – in long streets or terraces, or grouped in estates of detached and semi-detached houses, or blocks of flats. But every town – and most villages too – have houses of different *styles*. And the building *materials* are usually different.

Here is a picture-puzzle to start you off. The two pictures show houses built in different periods of history.

1 _____ **2** _____

1 From which period of history would you say these houses dated?
  medieval
  Tudor
  eighteenth century
  Victorian
  twentieth century

2 These materials have been used – thatch, brick, metal, wood, slate, stone, plaster. Find where the materials have been used.

Architectural styles

The styles of architecture of town houses – and country houses too – changed as time went on. The shape of the houses, the windows, doors, chimneys, roofs all altered to suit different needs.

It is possible for you to recognize *when* houses, terraces and flats were built by looking closely at their various features and the materials used in their construction – brick, stone, wood, slate, etc.

To help you with the next puzzle, here is a description of some of the architectural styles through the ages.

Saxon and Norman times (from 800 to 1300)   There are no houses from this period of history. Churches and castles that have survived were built solidly in stone.

Medieval houses (from 1300 onwards)   You can still see medieval houses at Lavenham in Suffolk and at other places. These are often 'half-timbered' houses with plaster filling between wooden columns and beams. The upper floors often overhang the ground floor.

Tudor (sixteenth century)   More solid houses with bay windows that were built out from the walls, tall chimneys and very small window panes (because glass was so expensive).

Queen Anne (early eighteenth century)   Often square in shape, with windows neatly placed in a symmetrical pattern. The doors were sometimes framed with columns and a *pediment* (a rounded or triangular arch over the door).

Regency (early nineteenth century)   The houses often had narrow or flat roofs. Windows were neatly proportioned, doors sometimes had overhead fanlights. Elegant terraces and crescents were built in this style at Bath, Edinburgh and other places.

Victorian (from 1840 onwards)   Town houses sometimes had tall chimneys like towers, slate roofs and small gardens enclosed by a stone wall. The houses themselves were solid, usually built in stone.

Edwardian (early twentieth century)   In the towns and cities, long terraces were built with two rooms 'up' and two rooms 'down' for city workers, and with large stone or brick houses for wealthier people.

Modern (twentieth century)   There are all kinds of styles to see. They include detached and semi-detached houses, large blocks of flats, terraces and bungalows.

Matching the styles

Now see if you can do this picture puzzle. There are eight different kinds of houses here. Match the drawings to the architectural style listed in the box.

1 _Queen Anne_ ✗
house

2 _medieval_ ✓

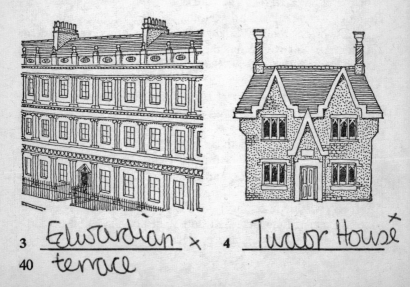

3 _Edwardian_ ✗
terrace

4 _Tudor House_ ✗

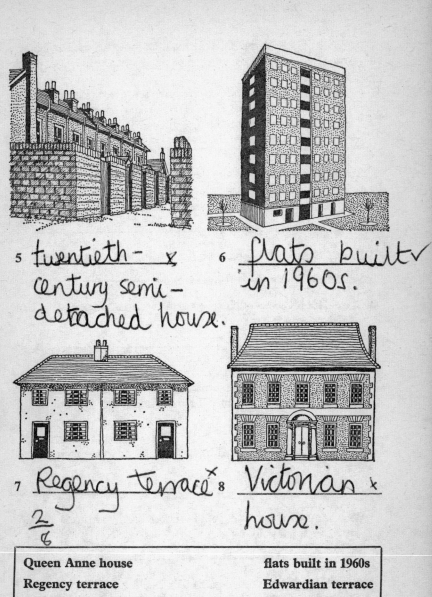

5 <u>twentieth-</u> ✗
century semi-
detached house.

6 <u>flats built</u> ✓
in 1960s.

7 <u>Regency terrace</u> ✗
$\frac{2}{6}$

8 <u>Victorian</u> ✗
house.

Queen Anne house	flats built in 1960s
Regency terrace	Edwardian terrace
Victorian house	medieval house
twentieth-century semi-detached house	Tudor house

What is it built of?

This section is about the different building materials used in houses. Tick the box when you see an example, and write in the space where you saw it.

1 Brick In the past, red bricks were often set in a zigzag or 'herring-bone' pattern and can still be seen in some old cottages. (Brick is used in many modern buildings, of course.)

☐ _____

2 Stone Sandstone and granite were used in medieval times for castles, and then in the eighteenth and nineteenth centuries for town houses, crescents and large country houses.

☐ _____

3 Flint Cottages were sometimes faced with flint set into cement.

☐ _____

4 Slate Houses were often given slate walls as well as slate roofs (especially in Wales).

☐ _____

5 Timber In the middle ages and in Tudor times, many houses and inns had a timber frame, usually painted black, with white plaster walls between the columns. They are said to be 'half-timbered'.

☐ _____

6 Tile Tiles were often nailed to wooden battens to keep out the cold and the rain.

☐ _____

7 Weather-boarding Overlapping timber boards are used to cover brick or stone walls.

☐ _____

8 Plaster Figures or patterns are often moulded in plaster on walls – the technical name is *plarge*. When the plaster is used to coat walls it is *stucco*.

☐ _____

Stone, brick, tile or slate?

Now match the materials or styles to the drawings. Write the correct word underneath the drawing.

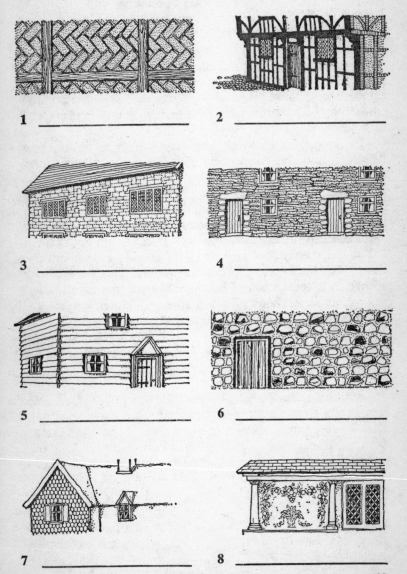

1 _____

2 _____

3 _____

4 _____

5 _____

6 _____

7 _____

8 _____

9 TOWNS

Most of us live in or near a town. But have you ever looked closely at the buildings ? They will tell you a lot about the history of the town and make your visit a lot more interesting.

As you walk about *your* town or one which you visit on holiday, look at the buildings. You might notice some very old churches, and perhaps a few built just over a hundred years ago. You should see large, important-looking buildings such as the town hall, the law courts, the library and so on. The fronts of shops will tell you another story. There might be old shops such as locksmiths and pawnbrokers, shops converted from houses, as well as new shopping precincts.

This section of the book will help you to recognize these buildings, and the quizzes and picture puzzles will test your knowledge and skill.

Buildings

Look carefully at the buildings in your town or the place you visit. Draw pictures and make notes to show some of the differences between various buildings.

You can usually spot schools, churches and factories straightaway. They are easy to pick out. But you will find that buildings change their uses. A row of houses in a street may have changed into ground-floor shops with flats upstairs. Houses, cinemas and sometimes churches have been converted into offices and factories. You might spot and make a note of buildings erected for special purposes – schools, workhouses, prisons, the police station, fire station and so on.

Streets

Street names also tell you a lot about the history of towns. A place may have a High Street, the old main street of the town. It may have a Cross Street where merchants once met to transact their business. It may have a Castle Street, a Priory Street, a Mill Road and a Quarry Road. These, and other names, give you the clues to unravel the mystery of the past.

Shops, markets and industries

Markets and local industries provide more clues. And the shops, both old and new, provide a lot of information for someone with sharp eyes. Now try these puzzles and quizzes and see how you get on.

Town picture quiz

Here is a picture quiz to test your knowledge of some of the older parts of towns. Match the pictures to the answers in the box below.

1 What do you think these posts were once used for?

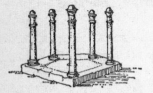

2 The White House at Dorking in Surrey is one of many reminders of travel in bygone days. What is the name given to these buildings?

3 Built by order of special town committees called Boards in the nineteenth century. But what is it?

4 Notice the round (sometimes square) solid building with no windows but with a heavy padlocked door. What is it?

5 This one (Walmgate in York) was a customs post during the day for traders who had to stop here and pay a toll on the goods they brought in. What is it called?

6 Supported on its solid wooden pillars, this one is at Ledbury in Herefordshire. What is it?

school	town jail	hitching-posts for horses
town gate	market hall	coaching inns

A word quiz on towns

You may come across these words in towns. But what do they mean?
Answer the quiz, using the words from the box.

buttercross	**gate**	**almshouse**	**Woolpack**
Glebe Street	**Chester**	**Bull Ring**	**guildhall**
Blackfriars	**cornhill**		

1 This town took its name from the Roman (Latin) word for a camp or walled town.

2 What was the name for the market where farmers sold their farm produce such as eggs, cheese and butter?

3 This inn took its name from the merchants who used it regularly. The inn name is very common in Yorkshire, Gloucestershire and Norfolk.

4 This name, which is used to describe a modern shopping area in a large city, was taken from a show which was open to the public, where animals were baited by dogs and men.

5 This part of the town or a street took its name from the land which once belonged to the church.

6 This word comes from the Danish for 'street' and is also used to describe entrances to the walls of ancient towns.

7 In this street or area of the town the traders and merchants who bought and sold grain had their stalls or shops.

8 At one time in this area there must have been a monastery run by monks of the Dominican Order.

9 A house built by the town council or by richer merchants for the old, sick or poor people.

10 This is where the town's craftsmen or merchants met to discuss the affairs of their business or trade.

Town puzzle corner

Use the clues to complete this word puzzle. The words are all names of town buildings.

1 m — — — — m
Most towns have one where they display historical exhibits.

2 w — — k — — — — e
In this building in Victorian times, the poor were given food and shelter.

3 a — c — — e
A covered-in shopping area with shops but no traffic.

4 i — — — — — — — y
Another name for a hospital.

5 e — — — — — — e
A building used for buying and selling goods such as cloth, coal, corn and wool.

6 w — — — h — — — e
A place to store goods such as grain and timber before they were sold.

Keeping a record

When you visit a town, keep a record of the buildings you see. Here is a list of buildings in towns. Write in the name of the town and street where you saw this building.

1 almshouses _____

2 town hall _____

3 guildhall _____

4 jail or prison _____

5 art gallery _____

6 library _____

7 exchange _____

8 university _____

9 hospital _____

10 cemetery _____

11 law courts _____

12 market hall _____

Draw a map of your town and mark on it the most important buildings. Make a list of curious street names in your town, and find their meanings.

Guildhalls and town halls

From the fifteenth century onwards, *town halls* were built by the Mayor and Corporation as places where they could discuss the town's business. *Guildhalls* were for meetings of groups of merchants of a particular trade who organized themselves into guilds. Later, some guildhalls found a new use as town halls.

In the nineteenth century, some cities in the north of England and in Scotland and Wales showed their new wealth by erecting fine public buildings such as town halls, libraries, art galleries, concert halls and museums. Sometimes these buildings were modelled on Roman and Greek temples, on palaces and castles, and even followed the style of a French castle, a *château*.

In some market towns, corn exchanges were set up as centres of trade. In other places, the town councils built swimming pools, law courts, colleges and schools, workhouses for the poor, and hospitals. Charity organizations also erected schools, hospitals and workhouses.

Now test your knowledge. Some of these buildings look similar but there are clues within them which will help you to match the drawing to the caption at the end.

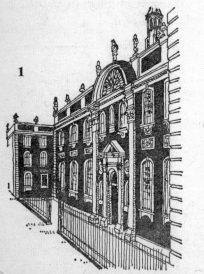

A Leeds Town Hall – notice the rows of steps, the columns at the entrance and the clock tower.

B The Guildhall at Worcester – built in the eighteenth century, with stone carvings, statues and pillars.

C The Portico Library, Manchester – built in the nineteenth century, it has a front like a Greek temple.

D A National school – built in the nineteenth century by the National Society, a charity organization.

E The Corn Exchange at Bury St Edmunds in Suffolk – notice the windows blocked in, the stone columns and parapet.

F The Law Courts at Birmingham – its turrets and pinnacles are like the skyline of a French château.

49

10 SHOPS AND MARKETS

Many towns began in the Middle Ages as places where people gathered to sell or exchange their goods. In those days shopping was done at fairs, and traders set up stalls in the market place or in side-alleys called 'rows'. Later on, many shopkeepers used the downstairs room of their house as a shop, with a sign outside the door to show their trade.

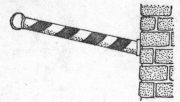

What kind of tradesman do you think used this sign? The answer is a *barber*. Barbers used also to be surgeons. Their sign was a pole with white and red stripes. The red was for blood and the white stood for bandages.

Here are some more shop signs. What trade do you think was carried on here?

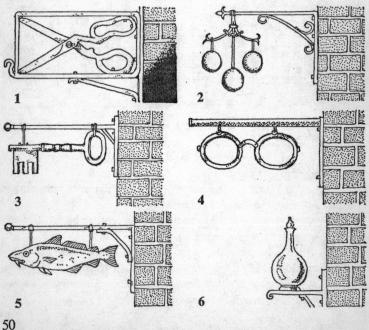

Inn signs

Wherever you go, you will see inns, taverns and 'pubs' (public houses). There are about 80,000 inns in Britain. Among the many different kinds of inn signs are soldiers, kings and queens, animals, birds, trades and occupations and many other subjects.

Suggest a name for these inns. Write your suggested name underneath the drawing.

1ᴬ The Keys + Lock.

2 The Swan + Ring

3 The Sailing Ship

4 The Jolly King

5 The Vice-Admiral

6 The Silent Cricketer.

7 The Cow's ring

8 The galloping horse.

The Windmill.

Market crosses and market halls

In some towns, you will find a large stone cross in the market place. This was set up to remind people that God was watching over and protecting the traders. (It was also hoped the cross would deter people from cheating or stealing!)

In the eighteenth century, some towns set up a more elaborate market cross built like a shelter with a roof over it. In other towns a market hall was erected. Sometimes these are simply open shelters supported by rows of pillars. In other towns a large market hall was built, where traders could set up their stalls protected from the wind and rain. On fine days the traders overflowed on to the market place outside.

Nearby, there might be a lock-up or jail for people who were awaiting trial. Around the market place there would be houses and an inn for travellers. These coaching inns (if the town was on a main road route) usually added extra rooms, stables and extra wide entrances to allow the coaches to pass through into the courtyard.

Look at the drawing of the market place in this town. Match the numbers on the drawing to the descriptions in the box.

the market cross	inn sign
a market hall	modern flats
a coaching inn	modern shops
traders' stalls	nineteenth-century shops
jail (with a clock and upper tower added later)	chapel

In the market place

11 MILLS AND FACTORIES

As you go around the countryside you will see many old industrial buildings which are linked to Britain's past. Among them are factories, mills, ironworks, collieries, railway stations and so on. People take a great interest in these old buildings. There may be a special kind of club or society in your area which arranges visits to look at these places. The name usually given to this kind of interest or study is industrial archaeology.

There are thousands of industrial buildings in Britain. Don't ignore them. They may not seem worth looking at, but if you examine them closely you will find some interesting facts.

What are these buildings? Can you name them? The clues should help.

1 Opened in 1781, it was the first in the world of its type.

_____

2 To use a stretch of road, travellers had to pay the keeper who lived in this.

_____

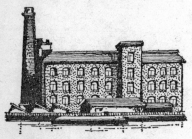

3 Near Manchester, this was built in the nineteenth century. It has a wharf where barges carrying the bales could tie up.

_____

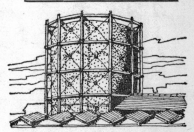

4 A framework of iron girders supports this and prevents the holder from toppling over.

_____

5 A large oven in Staffordshire, used to bake pots.

6 This type is called a 'smock' because the front of it looks like the garment once worn by farm-workers in the south of England. The building was used to grind corn.

7 In the nineteenth century, steam replaced water as the driving power for factory machinery. Built of brick or stone this was needed to carry away the smoke and fumes.

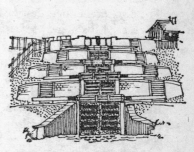

8 These are needed to allow canal boats to go uphill. Those in the picture are on the Bingley section of the Leeds and Liverpool Canal.

Which town, which building?

Match the towns, cities and other places in the box with the famous industrial building, bridge, canal, docks, etc., associated with it.

London	King's Lynn	Glasgow	Anglesey
Newcastle	Cardiff	Saltaire	Bristol
	Manchester	Coalbrookdale	

1 The Clifton Suspension Bridge, built across the Avon Gorge and designed by Isambard Kingdom Brunel, is nearby.

2 Here, in the Welsh Folk Museum at St Fagans, you can see farmhouses, a tannery, a working woollen mill, a tollhouse and other buildings, all restored to their original condition.

3 The St Katherine Dock, with cranes and dockside wharves, was built so that sailing ships could unload their cargoes here.

4 The Ship Canal, completed in 1894, linked this city to the coast and allowed a port to be built several miles from the sea.

5 Here are the warehouses, steelyards and homes built in the fifteenth century for merchants of the Hanseatic League who traded with German and Scandinavian ports.

6 The high level bridge, designed by George and Robert Stephenson, which carried a railway across the river Tyne, was opened in 1849.

7 At Port Dundas you can see the Forth and Clyde Canal with warehouses, bridges and aqueducts.

8 The Menai Suspension Bridge carries the road planned by Thomas Telford across the Menai Straits.

9 Here, beside the river Severn, is the place where you can see the blast furnace where Abraham Darby first smelted iron ore using coke.

10 Sir Titus Salt, Mayor of Bradford, built his own town here, with a huge woollen mill, houses for the workers, a hospital, school and library.

What are they?

Here are some things that were important in the past, but are rare now.

1 It's two things. In the first place it is a *bollard*, put up over 200 years ago to stop carts from climbing on to the kerb and breaking paving stones. But this bollard is rather special. It is made from an old gun. What kind of gun?

2 What is this vehicle? It's in a museum at Crich, Derbyshire. The museum is full of them from cities all over Britain. The only working ones now are in Blackpool, but at Crich and some other museums you can see and ride in one of these ancient vehicles. What is it?

3 In 1970 a famous ship returned to Bristol. It was designed by Isambard Kingdom Brunel, and launched in 1843. It was the first big merchant ship built of iron, and it had a screw propeller. It has been brought back from the Falkland Islands in the south Atlantic, and restored. What is its name?

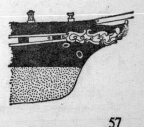

An industrial scene

Look at this drawing of an industrial scene. The labels have been missed out. Match the numbers on the drawing to the words in the box.

wool mill	canal	railway
viaduct	waterwheel	weavers' houses
engine house	winding wheel (for colliery)	
iron bridge	tollhouse	windmill

Masson Mill, Cromford

This is Masson Mill in Derbyshire, built by Sir Richard Arkwright, the cotton manufacturer. It was the first mill to use a water-wheel to drive the machinery for the spinning machines. The mill is of brick, with stone frames for the windows. The date 1769 is when the Arkwright firm was set up. The building itself dates from 1783.

If you go out exploring for buildings of the Industrial Revolution, here are some you might find. Keep a record in your notebook of where, and when, you saw these buildings.

Aqueduct	Ferry	Oil refinery	Shipyard
Beam engine	Flint-mill	Paper-mill	Slate quarry
Blast furnace	Forge	Piano factory	Steel-mill
Brewery	Gasworks	Post Office	Tin-mine
Brickworks	Glass works	Power station	Tollhouse
Bridge	Harbour	Printing works	Tramway
Canal	Ironworks	Quarry	Tunnel
Colliery	Lead-mine	Railway station	Waterwheel
Corn-mill	Lighthouse	Railway tunnel	Weavers' cottages or sheds
Cotton-mill	Lime-kiln	Railway viaduct	
Engine-house	Lock (canal)	Reservoir	Windmill
Factory	Milestone	Road bridge	Wool mill

59

12 STATUES AND MONUMENTS

Always keep your eyes open for statues and monuments. Here are some questions about some of the most famous in Britain.

1 Where is the statue of Eros?

2 What is the name of the admiral whose statue is at the top of a column in London?

3 Who is this famous archer whose statue is in Nottingham?

4 Which famous road in London, the route for ceremonial drives from Buckingham Palace, is overlooked by a statue of King George VI?

5 On the battlefield of Bannockburn, outside Stirling in Scotland, there is a statue of the Scottish leader on horseback. Who is he?

6 Who is the famous playwright whose statue is at Stratford-upon-Avon?

7 Which monument in London commemorates the dead of two World Wars?

8 Whose statue is this which stands in a square in Birmingham? The same lady asked for the Albert Memorial to be built in London in memory of her husband.

Keep a record. I saw famous statues at ....

....

....

13 ANSWERS

Discovering the Past
Page
5 1 barrow; 2 trackways; 3 keep; 4 Tower of London.

Ruins of Long Ago
6 1 Stonehenge; 2 Hadrian's Wall; 3 Silbury Hill; 4 Bath; 5 White Horse of Uffington; 6 Avebury.

9 1 four banks; 2 four ditches; 3 two gates.

10 1 a *road*, with a drainage grove down the centre, at Blackstone Edge in Lancashire; 2 a *tile-floor* or *mosaic*, with the head of a sea-god, from St Albans, Hertfordshire; 3 a *theatre*, also at St Albans; 4 a *wall-tower* at York.

11 1 main gate; 2 outer wall; 3 outer ditch; 4 bastions; 5 twelfth-century keep; 7 harbour; 9 twelfth-century church.

Castles and Forts
13 1 Tower of London; 2 Windsor Castle; 3 Hampton Court; 4 Edinburgh Castle.

14 1 Loch Leven; 2 Dover; 3 Caernarvon; 4 Berkeley; 5 Carisbrooke; 6 Goodrich; 7 Stirling; 8 Rochester.

15 1 well; 2 curtain wall; 3 drawbridge; 4 inner bailey; 5 battlements; 6 outer bailey.

18 1 portcullis; 2 battlements; 3 drawbridge; 4 curtain wall; 5 arrow slits; 6 barbican; 7 spiral staircase; 8 dungeon.

Churches and Cathedrals
20 1 altar; 2 pulpit; 3 pews; 4 nave; 5 chancel; 6 screen; 7 organ; 8 brasses.

21 1 fan vaults; 2 effigies; 3 lectern; 4 screen; 5 font; 6 piscina.

22 1 gargoyle; 2 belfry; 3 tower; 4 porch; 5 west door; 6 churchyard; 7 buttress; 8 pinnacle; 9 lych-gate; 10 weather-vane; 11 scratch-dial; 12 parapet; 13 gravestone; 14 yew tree; 15 churchyard cross.

24   **1** St Paul's, London; **2** Liverpool; **3** St Giles, Edinburgh; **4** Canterbury; **5** Salisbury; **6** Coventry; **7** Wells; **8** York.

26   **1** Saxon; **2** Decorated; **3** Norman; **4** Early English Gothic; **5** Perpendicular.

Abbeys and Priories

28   **1** abbot; **2** (a) St Dominic (b) St Benedict (c) St Francis; **3** cantor; **4** (a) dormitory (b) storage cupboard; **5** novices; **6** lay brothers; **7** Prime; **8** manuscripts.

29   **1** chapter house; **2** cloisters; **3** carrels; **4** almonry; **5** parlour; **6** infirmary; **7** gatehouse; **8** refectory; **9** dormitory; **10** warming room.

30   **1** church; **2** cloisters; **3** chapter house; **4** refectory; **5** kitchen; **6** dormitory; **7** infirmary hall.

31   **1** crypt; **2** nave; **3** pulpit; **4** cloisters; **5** night stairs; **6** Abbot's kitchen.

Historic Houses

32   **1** Sandringham; **2** Apsley House; **3** Christopher Wren; **4** Winston Churchill; **5** George Washington; **6** Macbeth.

33   **1** Berkeley Castle; **2** Speke Hall; **3** Royal Pavilion; **4** Castle Howard.

34   **1** Blenheim; **2** Hever Castle; **3** Hatfield House; **4** Abbotsford; **5** Ann Hathaway's Cottage; **6** Woburn Abbey.

35   **1** Holyrood; **2** Castle Howard; **3** Harewood House; **4** Warwick Castle; **5** Belvoir Castle; **6** Cardiff Castle; **7** Blenheim Palace; **8** Woburn Abbey; **9** Longleat House; **10** Beaulieu.

36   **1** Osborne House; **2** Glamis Castle; **3** Longleat House; **4** Chatsworth.

37   **1** Hampton Court; **2** Dove Cottage; **3** Chirk Castle; **4** Forde Abbey; **5** Alnwick Castle.

Houses and Homes

38   **1** medieval; **2** twentieth century.

40   **1** Tudor; **2** medieval; **3** Regency terrace; **4** Victorian house; **5** Edwardian terrace; **6** 1960s flats; **7** twentieth-century semi-detached; **8** Queen Anne house.

43   **1** brick; **2** timber; **3** stone; **4** slate; **5** weather-boarding; **6** flint; **7** tile; **8** plaster.

Towns

45   **1** hitching-posts for horses; **2** coaching inns; **3** school; **4** town jail; **5** town gate; **6** market hall.

46   **1** Chester; **2** buttercross; **3** Woolpack; **4** Bull Ring; **5** Glebe Street; **6** gate; **7** cornhill; **8** Blackfriars; **9** almshouse; **10** guildhall.

47   **1** museum; **2** workhouse; **3** arcade; **4** infirmary; **5** exchange; **6** warehouse.

48   **1** and B; **2** and C; **3** and E; **4** and F; **5** and A; **6** and D.

Shops and Markets

50   **1** tailor; **2** pawnshop; **3** locksmith; **4** optician; **5** fishmonger; **6** chemist.

51   **1** Crosskeys; **2** Swan; **3** Ship; **4** King's Head; **5** Lord Nelson; **6** Cricketer; **7** Bull; **8** Black Horse; **9** Windmill.

52   **1** jail (with a clock and upper tower added later); **2** market cross; **3** nineteenth-century shops; **4** traders' stalls; **5** coaching inn; **6** chapel; **7** market hall; **8** modern flats; **9** modern shops; **10** inn sign.

Mills and Factories

54   **1** iron bridge (at Coalbrookdale, Salop); **2** tollhouse; **3** cotton-mill; **4** gasometer; **5** kiln; **6** windmill; **7** chimney; **8** locks.

56   **1** Bristol; **2** Cardiff; **3** London; **4** Manchester; **5** King's Lynn; **6** Newcastle; **7** Glasgow; **8** Anglesey; **9** Coalbrookdale; **10** Saltaire.

57   **1** cannon; **2** tram; **3** *Great Britain*.

58   **1** canal; **2** winding wheel; **3** iron bridge; **4** wool mill; **5** tollhouse; **6** viaduct; **7** waterwheel; **8** windmill; **9** weavers' houses; **10** railway; **11** engine house.

Statues and Monuments

60   **1** Piccadilly Circus, London; **2** Nelson; **3** Robin Hood; **4** the Mall; **5** Robert Bruce; **6** William Shakespeare; **7** the Cenotaph; **8** Queen Victoria.